Introduction

Get ready to have some fun!

The lofty Blue Ridge Mountains of Northeast Georgia have long attracted throngs of visitors with their marvelous combination of enchanting beauty and spellbinding charm.

Two of the most popular destinations in Northeast Georgia are the mountain towns of Helen and Dahlonega. While these historic villages serve as gateways to the higher mountains beyond, each possesses its own unique character and charm.

A tremendous variety of attractions and recreational opportunities awaits the visitor to this splendid region.

When exploring an area that offers as much as this one, it can sometimes be a bit of a challenge just to decide *what* you want to see and do. Hopefully, that's where this little book comes in.

Dozens of beautiful, interesting and exciting destinations have been organized to give you just the right amount of information you need to make your visit to these wonderful mountains a bit more fun.

Stuff this little book into your purse or pocket while you're here. Wherever you happen to be, you're probably just around the corner from another great mountain destination!

A Word to the Wise about SAFETY!

While ever-increasing numbers of visitors flock to the Northeast Georgia mountains each year, the area nonetheless remains wild and potentially dangerous. Numerous deaths and hundreds of injuries occur each year because of accidents, poor preparedness, or downright stupid behavior.

Waterfall safety: By far the most dangerous attractions in the Northeast Georgia mountains are its waterfalls. Truly these wonders of nature are spectacular to behold. However, each year people are seriously injured or killed either attempting to climb up the banks or **on** the falls themselves. Please be content to view our waterfalls from the safety of observation decks or a safe area at the base.

General safety: Please obey all posted rules and regulations when in the Chattahoochee National Forest, state parks, recreation areas or wilderness areas.

If possible, do not hike alone, and always let someone else know where you are going and when you expect to return. If possible, carry a first-aid kit in a day-pack and know how to use it.

Be aware of changing weather conditions, especially the possibility of lightning during summer thunderstorms.

Always lock your automobile and store any valuables in the trunk where they cannot be seen. Safety first!

The
Helen – Dahlonega
Pocket Companion

Great ideas for fun day trips in the North Georgia mountains

compiled by Brian A. Boyd
Fern Creek Press • Clayton, Georgia

The Helen – Dahlonega Pocket Companion

ISBN #1-893651-05-3
Published and distributed by:
Fern Creek Publishing
PO Box 1322
Clayton, GA 30525
(706) 782-5379

Printed by Vaughan Printing
Nashville, Tennessee, USA

The author and publisher of this guidebook assume no responsibility for any loss of property, accident, injury or death sustained while visiting any of the locations described herein. Use all safety precautions and common sense when in the wild.

The Helen – Dahlonega Pocket Companion

Table of Contents

Section One

Touching the Past

Dahlonega Gold Museum
DESTINATION 1

Commemorates the site of America's first gold rush

Dahlonega Gold Museum State Historic Site – Lumpkin County
#1 Public Square, Dahlonega, GA 30533
Open 9 am to 5 pm
Sunday 10 am to 5 pm
(706) 864–2257

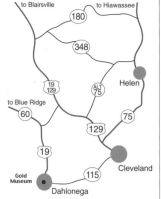

• **Small admission fee**

etween the years 1838 and 1861, more than $6 million worth of gold was coined by the US Mint located in the mountain boom town of Dahlonega. Today, visitors can explore the old Lumpkin County Courthouse and learn about this exciting time at the Dahlonega Gold Museum. Samples of gold nuggets and coins minted at the old US Mint in Dahlonega are on display, as are many photos from this rugged era. A short film teaches proper mining techniques, as well as providing a glimpse into the life of those rugged early gold-seekers. Come on by and catch the fever!

Stovall Mill Bridge

Covered bridges - a rare historical treasure

DESTINATION **2**

Stovall Mill Covered Bridge – White County
Sautee–Nacoochee Valley

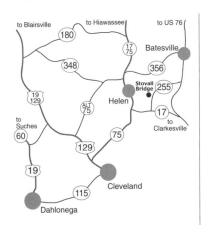

- **Good picnic spot**
- **Bring your camera**
- **Foot traffic only**

Once covered bridges were plentiful across Northeast Georgia, but only a precious few remain to this day. One of these is historic Stovall Mill Covered Bridge in the Sautee-Nacoochee valley. Built in 1895 by Will Purdue, this 37-foot long structure spans Chickamauga Creek, and is also known as Chickamauga Bridge.

Directions: From Helen, proceed south and turn onto Hwy 17 south. Drive several miles and turn onto Hwy 255 north. Drive 2.7 miles to the bridge on right.

White County Courthouse DESTINATION 3

Historic centerpiece of bustling White County

Located in the center of Cleveland's town square

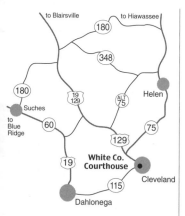

- **Normal hours open: Thursday, Friday and Saturday, 10 am – 3 pm**
- **(706) 865–3225**

According to local historians, slaves molded and fired the bricks which were used to build the historic White County Courthouse, nestled in the middle of the busy town square. Built between 1859-1860, the courthouse has been restored by the White County Historical Society.

Simplistic yet stately, the White County Courthouse beckons visitors to stop and explore, and makes a great starting point for any tour of this highly scenic and historically significant area.

Track Rock Gap

DESTINATION 4

Mysterious soapstone carvings of Native Americans

Track Rock Gap Archeological Area – Union County

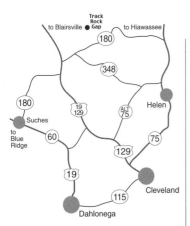

- **Ancient Indian petroglyphs**
- **Short walk**

For those visitors interested in the Native American history of the region, 52-acre Track Rock Archeological Area may be of particular interest. A number of soapstone boulders in this site feature ancient carvings called *petroglyphs*. These petroglyphs appear to resemble circles, crosses, bird tracks, animal tracks and even human footprints.

The Cherokee Indians referred to the Track Rock Gap area as *degayelunha* or "printed place". Footpaths lead past the boulders, which are now protected by metal cages to prevent them from being further vandalized.

Directions: From the junction of US 19/129 & GA 180, take 180 east to Town Cr. Rd. (1.5 miles beyond 348) on left. Go 2.2 miles, turn right onto Trackrock Church Rd. Go 3.1 miles to stop sign. Turn right on Trackrock Rd and go 0.8 mile to marker on left.

Nacoochee Valley

Beautiful mountain valley steeped in history

Nacoochee Valley – White County

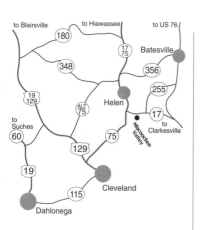

- Scenic drive
- Historic structures

The Unicoi turnpike, constructed between 1815 and 1817, was the first wagon road constructed across the imposing Southern Appalachian mountains. This rugged "highway" ran through beautiful Nacoochee Valley and the heart of the Cherokee Nation, which had thrived here for thousands of years.

In the years that followed, settlers began to build their homes and farms here. After the discovery of Gold in the area in 1838, the mining industry took over the valley, followed in the early 20th century by huge lumber companies.

Today, Nacoochee Valley still attracts attention, though it is now mainly residents and tourists who ply the turnpike. Thankfully, many of the historic structures of Nacoochee Valley have been preserved for current day education and enjoyment.

If you're interested in the early history of the valley, head south from Helen and turn onto Hwy 17. The 2.2 miles from this junction to Hwy 255 features numerous historic structures.

Nacoochee Indian Mound - Guarding the entrance to Nacoochee Valley from Hwy 75, this structure was the center of the ancient Cherokee town *Gauxule*, and was visited by Spanish explorer DeSoto in 1540. The mound is 190' long, 150' wide, and 20' high. A historical marker provides additional information.

Just across the highway from the Indian Mound is *West End*, a beautiful Italiante mansion built Colonel John "Captain" Nichols after the civil war. Nearby Anna Ruby Falls is named for Nichols' only daughter, Anna Ruby.

Continue east on Highway 17 and you will see historic structures such as **Crescent Hill Baptist Church**, **Nacoochee United Methodist Church**, and the **old trading post**, to name a few. Many of these buildings have historic markers telling of their important role in Nacoochee Valley's history. Keep driving and keep looking, as there's much more to see in this beautiful mountain valley.

Lake Winfield Scott

Section Two

State Parks & Recreation Areas

Unicoi State Park

DESTINATION

One of Georgia's most scenic state parks

Unicoi State Park – White County
PO Box 997 • Helen, GA 30545 (706) 878-3982
Located 2 miles northeast of Helen on GA 356

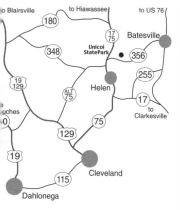

- **Boating, fishing & swimming**
- **Camping, cabins & lodge**
- **Hiking & picnicking**
- **User fee required**

Beautiful 1,081 acre Unicoi State Park has long been attracting thousands of visitors annually with its wide range of outdoor activities and accommodations. Whatever type of recreation you'd like to enjoy, chances are pretty good that you can do it at Unicoi State Park.

Accommodations: Unicoi features five camping areas with 84 tent, trailer and RV sites. If you'd like your visit to be a bit more civilized, 30 cottages and a 100 room lodge (with restaurant) are also available. Call 1-800-864-7275 for reservations.

Unicoi Lake: Beautiful 53-acre Unicoi Lake features its own sandy beach and swimming area. Canoe and paddle boat rentals are available.

Fishing: Trout fishing is a very popular activity in the park, both in Unicoi Lake and on Smith Creek, the lake's major tributary.

Picnicking: Numerous picnic areas are scattered around the park, including a number of covered shelters. Those wishing to reserve a shelter should call ahead.

Hiking: Unicoi features several hiking trails including the 2.4 mile **Unicoi Lake Trail**, the 1.3 or 2.6 mile **Bottoms Loop Trail**, the 3 mile **Unicoi/Helen Trail**, and the challenging 5 mile **Smith Creek Trail** which leads to Anna Ruby Falls.

Tennis: Four lighted courts are located near the lodge.

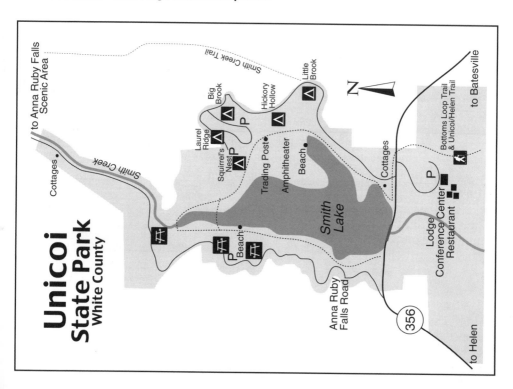

Vogel State Park

DESTINATION 7

Georgia's second oldest state park

Vogel State Park – Union County
7485 Vogel State Park Rd • Blairsville, GA 30152 (706) 745-2628
Located 3 miles north of Neel's Gap on US Hwy 19/129

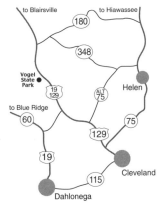

- **Boating, fishing & swimming**
- **Camping & cabins**
- **Hiking, picnicking & mini-golf**
- **Entrance fee required**

Georgia's second oldest state park was formed way back in 1928 when August Vogel donated a beautiful section of mountain property to the state. Today, magnificent 280-acre Vogel State Park is one of Georgia's most popular state parks.

Situated at a cool 2,500' elevation, Vogel can become quite crowded during the hot tourist season, so plan your trip to avoid busy weekends if possible. Vogel offers a wide variety of outdoor recreation, and is located close to dozens of mountain attractions.

Accommodations: Vogel State Park offers 95 tent and trailer camping sites complete with electrical hook-ups and water, and 15 primitive walk-in sites. A pioneer camping area is also available to groups by reservation only. Thirty-six rental cottages of varying sizes, each complete with kitchens and cookware, are available. Reservations may be made at 1-800-864-7275.

Trahylta Lake: Splashing Wolf Creek is stilled temporarily by cold, clear Lake Trahylta. This 22-acre gem features a swimming beach and bathhouse. Though private boats are not permitted on the lake, paddle boats are available. Fishing is also very popular here, as the lake is regularly stocked with trout.

Picnicking: Four picnic shelters and 65 picnic tables make Vogel a favorite place for this important mountain ritual. Call ahead to reserve a shelter.

Hiking: Vogel offers visitors four very different hiking opportunities. Two easy hikes include the one-mile **Trahylta Lake Trail** and the 0.6 mile **Byron Reece Nature Trail.** Offering more of a challenge are the 4 mile **Bear Hair Trail**, and the strenuous 12.5 or 13.5 mile **Coosa Backcountry Trail** (permit required), which features a 2,000' elevation gain.

Wolf Creek – Vogel State Park

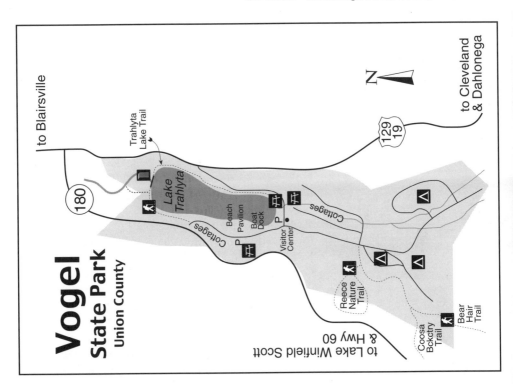

Amicalola Falls State Park DESTINATION 8

Georgia's gateway to the Appalachian Trail

Amicalola Falls State Park – Dawson County
Star Route, Box 215 • Dawsonville, GA 30534 (706) 265–4703
Located 20 miles west of Dahlonega on Hwy 52

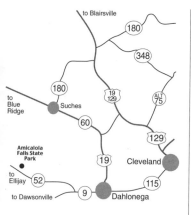

- **Camping, cottages & lodge**
- **Hiking, fishing & picnicking**
- **Entrance fee required**

Appropriately called *Ama kalola*, or "tumbling waters" by the native Cherokee, this sparkling cascade is the centerpiece for this 1,020-acre state park known as the southern base of the Appalachian Trail.

Accommodations: Amicalola Falls State Park offers a wide variety of facilities for the overnight visitor. For the more civilized, the 57-room lodge located near the brink of the falls offers several sizes. The park also features 17 campsites with water and electricity, and 14 fully equipped cottages. Call 1-800-864-7275 for camping reservations.

Picnicking: Five shelters and dozens of tables are available. Call ahead of time to reserve a shelter.

Hiking: The most notable hiking trail is the 8.1 mile blue-blazed **Appalachian Approach Trail** leading up to the Appalachian Trail at Springer Mountain. This trail is rated MODERATE to STRENUOUS, and is generally not for beginning hikers.

The 1.2 mile **West Ridge Trail** begins across the street from the Visitor Center, and makes for a nice nature walk. The most dramatic path in the park is the short 0.25 mile **Falls Trail** which leads up to the base of the falls.

Fishing: Fishing is permitted in the reflection pool below the falls and in Little Amicalola Creek during trout season.

Len Foote Hike Inn: Perfect for those who like to hike, but want to hit a nice soft mattress at the end of the trail. Hike

Inn is reached via an EASY to MODERATE five mile hike. Springer Mountain, southern terminus of the Appalachian Trail is located only 4.5 miles from the inn. Rates include private room with shower, dinner and breakfast. Call (404) 656-3530 for a brochure or call 1-800-864-7275 for reservations.

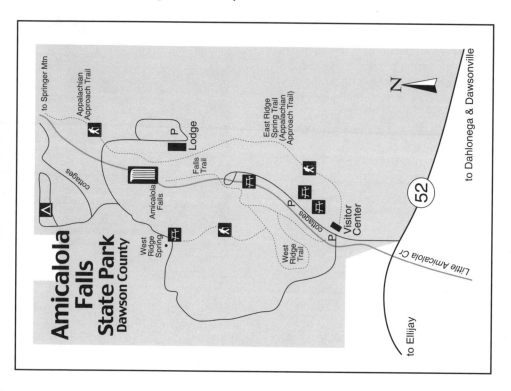

Andrews Cove

Convenient camping site with Appalachian Trail access

Andrews Cove Recreation Area – White County
Chattahoochee National Forest

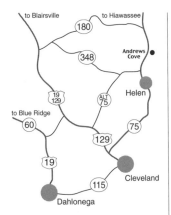

Tiny Andrews Cove Recreation Area is located just south of Unicoi Gap and the Appalachian Trail. This heavily wooded cove is bisected by scenic Andrews Creek. Only 10 campsites are available here, creating a somewhat intimate setting within the shady, lush cove. The 2 mile Andrews Cove Trail runs northeast from the cove up to the AT and FS 283 at Indian Grave Gap (2.7 miles from Unicoi Gap, 2.5 miles to Tray Mountain summit). Andrews Cove is a good camping spot for those looking for a small campground in a forest setting, but still relatively close to town.

Directions: From Helen, follow GA 75 north for 5 miles. Andrews Cove Recreation Area is located in a sharp hairpin turn on the right.

- **Hiking access to A.T.**
- **10 campsites**
- **User fee**

Smithgall Woods –
Dukes Creek Conservation Area

DESTINATION **10**

Smithgall Woods–Dukes Creek Conservation Area – White County
61 Tsalaki Trail • Helen, GA 30545   (706) 878–3087
Hours vary – please call

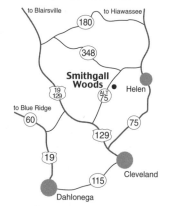

- **Hiking & Biking**
- **Trout Fishing & Hunting**
- **Picnicking & Wildlife Viewing**
- **Guided Tours & Educ. Programs**
- **Lodge**

Recently dedicated as a Georgia Heritage Preserve, the Smithgall Woods-Dukes Creek Conservation Area was acquired in 1994 from Charles A. Smithgall, Jr., noted conservationalist and businessman.

This spectacular 5,604-acre preserve features sparkling Dukes Creek, noted trout stream, as its crown jewel. Trout fishing is allowed on Dukes Creek, but it is catch-and-release only, with special regulations. Currently, trout fishing is allowed on Wednesday, Saturday and Sunday only.   Special quota hunts are conducted during the spring, fall and winter.

Currently, four miles of splendid hiking trails and eighteen miles of roadways lace

Smithgall Woods, providing hikers and bikers with plenty of avenues to explore this highly scenic area. Primitive group camping is also available.

Wildlife lovers will particularly enjoy visiting one of the planted food plots. These areas attract a wide variety of wildlife. Wildlife viewing stands have also been constructed to allow visitors the opportunity of observing native species in their own environment.

Smithgall Woods features an elegant cabin-style lodge which can accomodate only 28 guests. Rates can be acquired by calling (706) 878-3087, and include accomodations, meals and leisure/ interpretive activities.

Shuttle service and guided tours are available, but only on certain days of the week. Visitors desiring these services should call ahead for the current schedule or to make reservations.

All visitors to Smithgall Woods must register at the visitor center.

Directions: Smithgall Woods-Dukes Creek Conservation Area is located on GA Hwy 75-Alt, 3 miles west of Helen, just south of the Richard Russell Scenic Highway.

Smithgall–Woods Hiking Trail

Dockery Lake

DESTINATION 12

Six-acre mountain lake offers a wide variety of recreational opportunities

Dockery Lake Recreation Area – Lumpkin County
12 miles north of Dahlonega

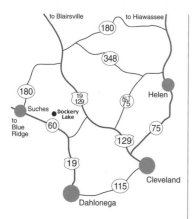

- **Hiking & Camping**
- **Picnicking & Fishing**
- **User fee required**
- **Appalachian Trail access**

Beautiful six-acre Dockery Lake lies situated in a peaceful wooded cove at an altitude of 2,388'. Its cold, clear mountain waters attract trout fishermen, while its intimate camping and picnicking facilities (11 campsites, 6 picnic tables) attract others seeking peace and quiet amidst this beautiful setting.

Two hiking paths of note begin in the parking area at Dockery Lake Recreation Area. The popular **Lakeshore Trail** (0.5 mile) is an easy loop trail which circles the lake and is handicap accessible.

The 3.4 mile **Dockery Lake Trail** provides access to the Appalachian Trail and is much more challenging. This path follows the remnants of an old logging road north to Miller Gap (2,980') on the Appalachian Trail. Though the net elevation gain is only about 600', the trail does a good bit of alternate climbing and descending. This includes a descent to Waters Creek (around 2,000' elevation), then a heart-pumping 0.5 mile climb before the grade eases up. The intersection with the Appalachian Trail lies 3 miles north of Woody Gap and 8.6 miles south of Neel's Gap.

The Dockery Lake Trail provides excellent opportunities to observe many of the flowering shrubs and wildflowers in the area. Laurel and rhododendron are quite common, and a wide variety of wildflowers bloom in the spring. Wildlife sightings are quite common as well. A multitude of bird species are found here, and deer are frequently sighted in the area, along with an occasional (but rare) black bear.

Directions: From Dahlonega take GA 60 north 12.3 miles. Turn right onto FS 654 and follow for 1 mile.

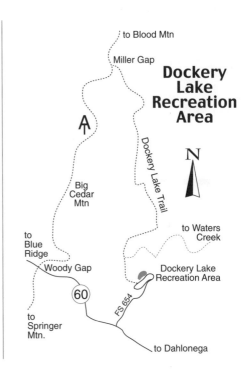

From the Dockery Lake Trail

Lake Winfield Scott

DESTINATION **12**

One of North Georgia's most scenic mountain lakes

Lake Winfield Scott Recreation Area – Union County
Chattahoochee National Forest

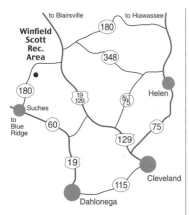

Beautiful 18-acre Lake Winfield Scott is the centerpiece of this easily accessible recreation area. Besides camping, fishing and picnicing, several hiking trails originate here. The 0.4 mile **Winfield Scott Trail** circles the lake, while the **Slaughter Creek Trail** (2.7 miles) and the **Jarrard Gap Trail** (1.2 miles) climb from the recreation area to the AT, creating several possibilities for Blood Mtn hikes.

Directions: The recreation area is located on Hwy 180, seven miles west of Hwy 19/ 129 and Vogel State Park.

- **Picnicing & group shelters**
- **Three hiking trails**
- **36 campsites**
- **Fishing**

Woody Gap

DESTINATION **13**

Roadside recreation Area offers picnicking and AT access

Woody Gap Recreation Area – Lumpkin County
Chattahoochee National Forest

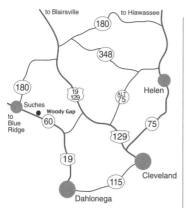

Woody Gap Recreation Area is bisected by the historic Appalachian Trail, and provides access for hikes in both directions. This tiny recreation area is a great site for roadside picnics, with tables nestled on both sides of GA 60 providing peaceful vistas south into Yahoola Valley.

Directions: Woody Gap Recreation Area is located 14 miles north of Dahlonega on GA Hwy 60 (5.4 miles north of the Hwy 19/60 split).

- **Picnicking**
- **Toilet facilities**
- **Scenic Views**
- **Hiking**

Waters Creek

DESTI**14**TION

Located along one of Northeast Georgia's trophy trout streams

Waters Creek Recreation Area – Lumpkin County
Adjacent to Chestatee Wildlife Management Area

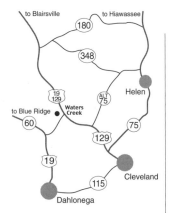

Located alongside splashing Waters Creek, and adjacent to the popular Chestatee Wildlife Management Area, this small recreation area is very popular with fishermen who come to test their skill on this carefully managed trophy trout stream.

This cozy spot features picnic tables, eight campsites, drinking water and toilet facilities. Several low, broad waterfalls on Waters Creek are visible from the road - the first is 1.2 miles from the highway; the second, 2.8 miles in. A series of cascades on Blood Mountain Creek is reached from a short trail 4.6 miles from the highway.

Directions: Waters Creek Recreation Area is located 12 miles north of Dahlonega on US 19. Watch for the signs and turn onto Dick's Creek Road (FS 34) and proceed one mile to the recreation area.

- **Camping**
- **Trophy trout fishing (note special regulations)**
- **Picnicking**
- **User fee charged**

Lake Chatuge

DES**15**TION

Recreation Area offers access to beautiful 7,000 acre TVA lake

Lake Chatuge Recreation Area – Towns County

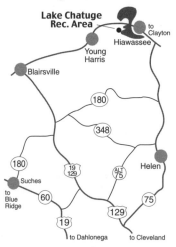

- **Camping & Hiking**
- **Fishing**
- **Boat ramp**
- **User fee required**

Massive 7,000-acre Lake Chatuge is a perfect destination for visitors who want to get out and enjoy a big body (of water, that is). This TVA impoundment nearly surrounds the town of Hiawassee, and offers great fishing and pleasure boating.

The recreation area is just minutes from scenic Hiawassee, and offers 30 campsites with toilets and showers. A boat ramp provides lake access. The **Lake Chatuge Loop Trail** winds around the peninsula for 1.2 scenic miles. Inquire locally for boat rentals.

Directions: Take US 76 west from Hiawassee for 2 miles. Turn left onto GA 288 and proceed 1 mile to the recreation area.

Section Three

Classic Walks

Brasstown Bald

Georgia's highest peak offers magnificent views

Brasstown Bald (4,784')
Brasstown Bald Recreation Area – Towns County
Brasstown Wilderness – Towns and Union Counties

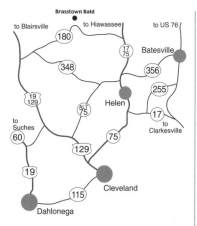

- **Hiking Trails & picnicking**
- **Visitor Center & Exhibits**
- **User fee required**

Rising to a majestic height of 4,784', Brasstown Bald is the highest peak in the North Georgia mountains. Though surrounded by the rugged 12,600+ acre Brasstown Wilderness, Brasstown Bald is easily accessible to visitors via GA 180 Spur which climbs to within 0.5 mile of the summit.

The unusual name "Brasstown" is said to come from a misunderstood translation. The Cherokee Indians called the area *Itse' yi*, which means "new green place". Early settlers to the region evidently mistook it for *Untsai' yi*, which means "brass".

From the parking area, visitors may choose to visit the summit by hiking up a 0.5 mile paved trail (MODERATE difficulty) or pay a nominal fee to ride in a van which is operated by a concessionaire.

The US Forest Service operates a visitor center at the summit which features exhibits on the history and ecology of the Brasstown Bald area. Be sure to view the short video which is shown at regular intervals during the day.

Atop the visitor center adjacent to the fire tower is a large circular observation platform offering a dramatic view of the North Georgia region. If conditions are favorable, visitors can see well into North Carolina and Tennessee.

Hiking: Several hiking trails connect with the parking area at Brasstown Bald, providing numerous challenging routes to the summit from points in the area. The **Arkaquah Trail** descends from the parking area west for 5.5 miles to Trackrock Gap on Trackrock Road.

The 7 mile **Wagon Trail** runs north to Young Harris College, and the **Jack's Knob Trail** runs south along a ridgeline to Jack's Gap at GA 180 before rising to the Appalachian Trail at Chattahoochee Gap.

Directions: From Helen, follow GA 75 north for approximately 12 miles. Turn left onto GA 180 and proceed 6 miles to GA 180 spur.

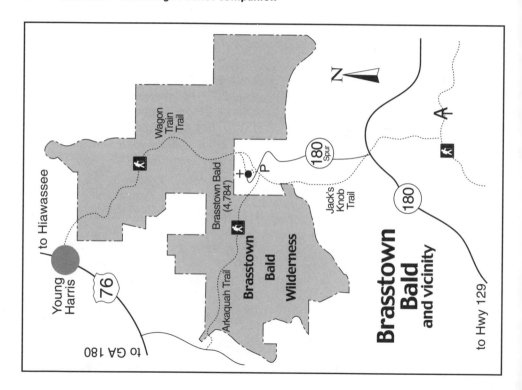

Blood Mountain

DESTINATION **17**

Popular summit destination via the Appalachian Trail

Blood Mountain Wilderness Area – Union County
Length: 4.4 miles to 6.5 miles depending on route
Hike is rated MODERATE to STRENUOUS

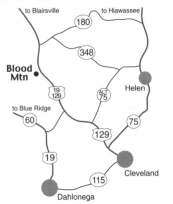

- **Limit groups to 12 persons or less**
- **Day hikers use the Reece Spur Trail**
- **Do not park vehicles at Neel's Gap**
- **Walasi–Yi outfitters store**

For years Blood Mountain has been one of North Georgia's most popular day hikes - and for good reason. From Neel's Gap, the closest direct route to the summit, the renowned Appalachian Trail ascends 1,500 heart-pounding vertical feet. Legend has it that Blood Mountain attained its graphic moniker from a bloody Indian conflict centuries ago, but the only battle taking place here today is the one you'll wage as you climb to the 4,461' summit.

Day hikers are required to park at the Reece Picnic Area (elev. 3,000') and hike the spur trail 0.4 mile up to Flatrock Gap (3,460'). From here hikers may choose to ascend directly to the summit, another 1.5 miles distant, or create a loop hike by following the 1.8 mile **Freeman Trail** along the southern flank of Blood's summit to another junction with the A.T.

A right turn here offers a nice loop over the mountain's summit and back to the parking area. At a lofty 4,461', Blood's summit offers sublime views from a number of boulder piles and rocky outcrops. An old hiking shelter built by the Civilian Conservation Corps in the 1930's offers overnight hikers a respite from their tents, space permitting.

The summit is particularly alluring in the late spring and early summer when laurel, rhododendron and wildflowers compete with the serene views for your attention. Note: Nearby Lake Winfield Scott (via the **Slaughter Gap Trail**), Big Cedar Mountain (via the AT) and the **Duncan Ridge Trail** are other good options for day hikes here.

Visitors should be aware that Blood Mountain is a very popular destination in the warmer months. The summit can become congested with hikers, particularly on the weekends. If possible, plan your hike in the early morning, where the chances of solitude are much higher.

While several springs do normally occur along the trail, do not depend on them. Always bring plenty of water, particularly on a demanding summit hike.

Be sure to drop by and visit Walasi-Yi in Neel's Gap. Besides offering expert backpacking advise and equipment, the view from their picnic area is outstanding. The Appalachian Trail passes right through a breezeway here.

Directions: Neel's Gap is located along Hwy 19/129 approximately 18 miles north of Cleveland, and 21 miles north of Dahlonega.

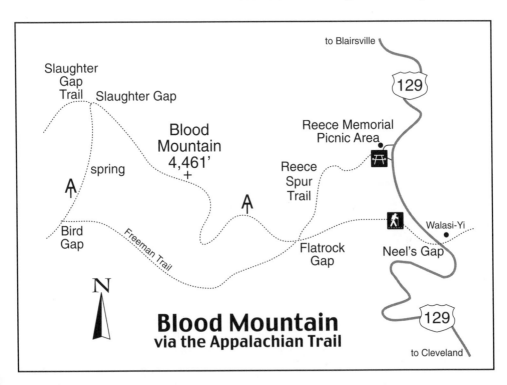

Blood Mountain
via the Appalachian Trail

Tray Mountain

via the Appalachian Trail

DESTINATION **18**

Tray Mountain (4,430') via the Appalachian Trail
Tray Mountain Wilderness Area – White County
Length: 1.8 miles round trip
Hike is rated MODERATE

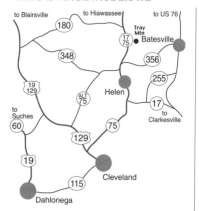

- **Excellent scenic vistas**
- **Botanically rich area**

Tray Mountain offers one of the most dramatic short hikes to an Appalachian summit to be found anywhere, and can be enjoyed by almost anyone in reasonably good shape. From the intersection of FS 698 and FS 79, it is a 0.9 mile walk to the summit. There is a 600' change in elevation along the way - just enough to make you feel like you've earned your reward once at the top.

Most of the climb is negotiated via broad, looping switchbacks, allowing hikers the opportunity to fully enjoy the beautiful hardwood forest. Several small overlooks are passed along the way, providing a tease of the bigger views just ahead.

The actual summit (4,430') is small, very unlike Blood Mountain, Tray's cousin to the southwest. Though there's not a lot of room to spread out, there is a great deal of scenery to enjoy. Nearby high peaks such as Blood Mountain and Brasstown Bald, Georgia's highest mountain, rise dramatically from the dense forests. To the south, the unmistakable profile of Mt. Yonah, the highest point in the Georgia Piedmont, is visible just north of Cleveland. To the east, several narrow arms of beautiful Lake Burton stand out. On an extremely clear day, Atlanta's Stone Mountain can even be glimpsed.

The Tray Mountain summit can be quite congested in the warmer months, especially on the weekends. If you find the summit occupied, try walking an additional few hundred yards to the north. A side trail branches to the right from the AT out to an excellent southern overlook.

Directions: It will probably take you more time to reach the trailhead than it takes to walk to the top. The recommended route is to take Hwy 75 north from Helen for 11 miles and turn right on FS 283 (2 miles north of Unicoi Gap). This is the road for High Shoals Scenic Area. Proceed 4 bumpy miles, then turn east (left) onto FS 79. Proceed for 2 miles to junction with FS 698 and the Appalachian Trail.

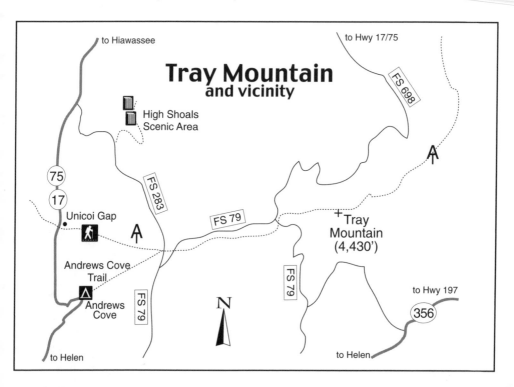

Raven Cliffs Trail

Beautiful scenic hike along a splendid, cascading stream

Raven Cliffs Wilderness Area – White County
2.5 miles (one way) to cliffs and falls
Hike is rated MODERATE

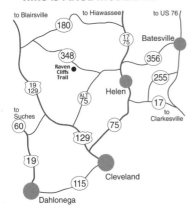

- **Highly scenic area**
- **Numerous small waterfalls**
- **Outstanding flora**
- **Use extreme caution at cliffs**

The beautiful 9,649-acre Raven Cliffs Wilderness Area is home to several outstanding trails, including several miles of the Appalachian Trail. None, however, is any more scenic than the popular **Raven Cliffs Trail**, a 2.5 mile stroll terminating at massive Raven Cliffs.

This blue-blazed trail originates at an unmarked parking area, following Dukes Creek downstream for 150 yards before angling to the right and proceeding upstream along splashing Dodd's Creek. Three minor falls are encountered along the way, including a 12' drop at mile 1.0, and an impressive 25' drop about 1.5 miles from the trailhead. Keep going, as these only serve to whet your appetite.

At mile 2.5, hikers encounter the 90' high grey cliff face punctuated with a narrow vertical cleft. Within this split Dodd Creek pours straight down into a dark pool, creating one of the most unusual waterfalls in North Georgia. Though the creek is relatively small here, the combination of natural elements produces an eerily dramatic effect.

From the base of the cliffs, a steep, root-grabbing climb takes you to the top of the cliffs **(extreme caution - steep cliff faces - definitely not for children)** where an upper cascade pours directly behind, then through, the cliff face.

The Raven Cliffs Trail has always been a favorite, and can become crowded during peak times. Try to plan a visit here early in the day, particularly on a weekday, if possible. The magic of Raven Cliffs is even more special if you are able to enjoy it in solitude.

Directions: From the junction of GA 75 ALT and GA 348 (Russell Hwy), proceed north for 2.5 miles to the large gravel pull-off on the right. The trailhead is not very noticeable, unless it is packed with cars.

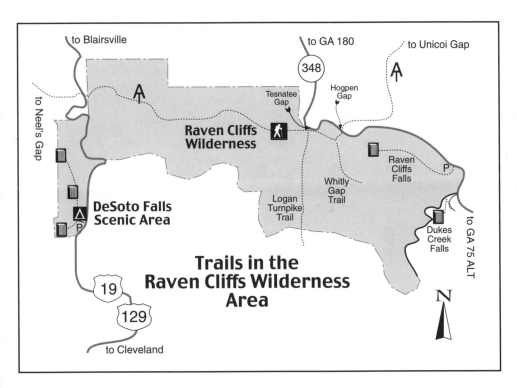

to Blairsville

to GA 180

to Unicoi Gap

348

to Neel's Gap

Raven Cliffs Wilderness

Tesnatee Gap

Hogpen Gap

DeSoto Falls Scenic Area

P

Raven Cliffs Falls

P

Whitly Gap Trail

Logan Turnpike Trail

Dukes Creek Falls

to GA 75 ALT

Trails in the Raven Cliffs Wilderness Area

19

129

to Cleveland

N

Big Cedar Mountain

Short hike on Appalachian Trail offers tall views

Big Cedar Mountain (3,737') via the Appalachian Trail
Chattahoochee National Forest – Lumpkin County
Length: 2 miles round trip
Hike is rated MODERATE

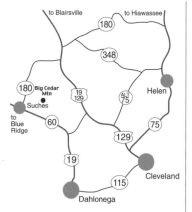

- **Great picnic spot**
- **Scenic Views**

The summit of Big Cedar Mountain is a moderately easy destination reached via the Appalachian Trail north of Woody Gap (3,160'). Actually, the first 0.7 mile is more of a stroll than a hike, as the trail climbs less than 200'. The final segment switchbacks up to a large open rock outcrop known as "Preacher's Rock" which provides great views of the Waters Creek watershed to the south. The actual summit is heavily wooded and doesn't offer much in the way of views, but "the rock" is a great place to linger.

Directions: The Woody Gap trailhead is located 14 miles north of Dahlonega on GA Hwy 60 (5.4 miles north of the Hwy 19/60 split).

Sosebee Cove

DESTINATION 21

Stroll through a beautiful cove of giant hardwoods

Sosebee Cove Scenic Area– Union County
175–acre scenic area

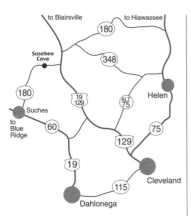

- **Great short hike**
- **Botanically rich area**

A scenic 0.5 mile trail circles this 175-acre scenic area, set-aside as a memorial to Arthur Woody, known as the "Barefoot Ranger." Ranger Woody served with the Forest Service from 1911 to 1945, and was instrumental in securing the purchase of the cove by the Forest Service. The cove is famous for its stand of huge yellow poplar and wide variety of wildflowers and ferns.

Directions: From the intersection of Hwy 19/129 and GA 180, proceed west on GA 180 for two miles to the parking area.

Wildcat Mountain

Whitly Gap Trail traverses a beautiful mountain ridge

Wildcat Mtn. (3,730') via the Whitly Gap Spur Trail
Raven Cliffs Wilderness Area – White County
0.7 mile (one way) to summit; 1.1 miles (one way) to Whitly Gap
Hike rated MODERATE (300' elevation gain)

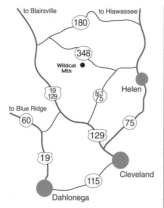

- Picnic spot
- Scenic views
- See map on page 47

This beautiful spur trail leads from the Appalachian Trail south along a beautiful narrow ridgeline to the scenic summit of Wildcat Mountain. The initial 0.25 mile from Hogpen Gap to the spur trail is the most strenuous part of this climb. The half-mile stroll to the summit traverses a beautiful area lined with moss covered rocks and through thick tunnels of rhododendron. Views from the top are excellent. The Whitly Gap shelter is another 0.6 mile distant, but the rest of the trail doesn't live up to the beauty of the first half-mile.

Directions: From the junction of GA 75 ALT and GA 348 (Russell Hwy), proceed north for 7 miles to Hogpen Gap at the White/Union County line. Follow the Appalachian Trail south for 0.25 mile to the Whitly Gap Spur Trail.

Logan Turnpike Trail

DESTINATION **23**

Early toll road used during pioneer days

Raven Cliffs Wilderness Area – White County
2 miles (one way)
Hike rated MODERATE to STRENUOUS (1,300' elevation change)

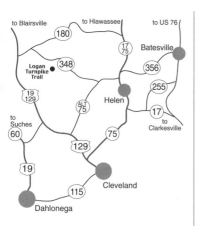

- **Scenic short hike**
- **Historical significance**
- **See map on page 47**

For those who complain about traveling across the country by automobile, the **Logan Turnpike Trail** may provide a little perspective. This trail traces the route of an early toll road through the area. The term "road" is used loosely, as the trail is not only very rough and rocky, but also extremely steep in the first half-mile below Tesnatee Gap. About 0.2 mile below the southern end of the trail on Town Creek Road (gravel) is the old tollkeeper's residence (designated by historical marker). This hike combines history, scenery and some strenuous walking.

Directions: The trailhead is located along the Russell Hwy (348) in Tesnatee Gap, 7.6 miles north of GA 75 ALT. The trail begins on the north side of the small parking area - look for the wooden marker.

The Long Trails

DESTINATION 24

Appalachian Trail, Benton MacKaye Trail and Duncan Ridge Trail

Trails located generally northwest of Dahlonega and Helen
Recommended for experienced hikers

local sources for information:

Walasi–Yi (Neel's Gap at AT)
(706) 745-6095

Amicalola Falls State Park
Dawsonville, GA
(706) 265-4703

Appalachian Outfitters
Dahlonega, GA
(706) 867-6677

Hard core hikers may not be satisfied with some of the shorter day trips listed in a guide of this type. Not to worry, however, as it is only a short drive from Dahlonega and Helen to segments of three of the "long trails" of the region.

Appalachian Trail in Georgia - from Springer Mountain to Bly Gap (NC line) 75 miles. Numerous day hikes available.

Benton MacKaye Trail - named for the "father of the Appalachian Trail", this 78 mile trail runs from Springer Mountain to the Tennessee line in the Cohutta Wilderness.

Duncan Ridge Trail - follows the longest continuous ridge off the Blue Ridge. From Springer Mountain to Slaughter Gap near Blood Mountain (31 miles).

Several excellent guides detail these long trails.

Section Four

4

The Magic of Falling Waters

Anna Ruby Falls

Rare twin cascade is one of Georgia's most beautiful

Anna Ruby Falls Recreation Area – White County
0.4 mile walk along paved trail to falls
Easy to Moderate

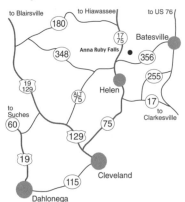

- **Visitor Center (706) 878-3574**
- **Picnicking**
- **Gift shop and restrooms**
- **Entrance fee required**

Beautiful Anna Ruby Falls, born at the junction of cascading York and Curtis Creeks, would be high on anyone's list of *must-see* destinations in the Helen area. This magnificent twin waterfall is named for Anna Ruby Nichols, the only daughter of Colonel John H. Nichols. Nichols was an early Nacoochee Valley land owner and the builder of the magnificent Victorian mansion *West End*, located just across Highway 17 from the Nacoochee Indian Mound.

The 1,600-acre Anna Ruby Falls Scenic Area was established in 1964, and rapidly became one of the most popular natural destinations in the North Georgia Mountains.

To reach Anna Ruby, visitors must follow a paved 0.4 mile trail to a large observation deck at the base of the double drop. Along the way, crashing Smith Creek provides plenty of entertainment. Interpretive markers provide information into the history, plant life and wildlife of the area.

The view from the observation platform is spellbinding. To your left, Curtis Creek slides 153 feet down a steep rock face. To the right, York Creek drops an abrupt 50 feet. Here, on the southern slopes of lofty Tray Mountain, these two streams merge into cascading Smith Creek, source of beautiful Unicoi Lake just a few miles downstream.

The **Chattahoochee-Oconee Heritage Association** operates a gift shop adjacent to the parking area.

Additionally, the 4.6 mile **Smith Creek Trail** connects the falls with Unicoi State Park, and the **Lion's Eye Trail** (by the picnic area) is designed for blind and visually impaired visitors.

Directions: From Helen, take GA 75 north for one mile. Turn right onto GA 356 and proceed 1.5 miles. Turn left at sign and proceed 3.6 miles to the parking area.

Amicalola Falls

Georgia's tallest cascade

Amicalola Falls State Park – Dawson County
Viewable from parking area or via 0.25 mile trail to base

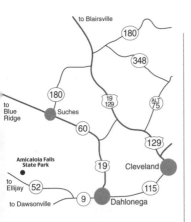

Recognized as the highest waterfall in Georgia, Amicalola Falls is the centerpiece of this popular state park about 20 minutes west of Dahlonega. Official measurements put Amicalola's height at 729', though only the top several hundred feet are easily visible. Follow the trail from the base to several viewing platforms below the upper cascades for a close-up view.

Directions: Amicalola Falls State Park is located on Hwy 52, 18 miles west of Dahlonega.

- Great picnic spot
- See Amicalola Falls State Park section on page 24 for more information

Cane Creek Falls

DESTINATION **27**

Privately owned cascade is just a few minutes from town

**Camp Glisson – Lumpkin County
2 miles north of Dahlonega
(706) 864–6181**

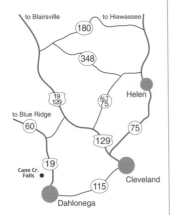

- **Short stroll**
- **Bring your camera**

Visitors to Dahlonega who want a taste of scenic beauty while staying close to town should visit lovely Cane Creek Falls on the grounds of Camp Glisson, a United Methodist facility. This wide 30' cascade spills into a large pool, and except during extreme dry spells, is a surprisingly large waterfall. Guests should be aware that the camp is closed to the public when camp is in session.

Directions: From downtown Dahlonega, head north on GA 60 Business spur for 2 miles. Turn left onto Cane Creek Rd and proceed 0.8 mile to the camp. The parking area for the falls is to the right.

Dukes Creek Falls

Enjoyable walk to the base of an alluring cascade and stream

Dukes Creek Falls Recreation Area – White County
Length: 2.2 miles round trip to falls
Hike is rated MODERATE

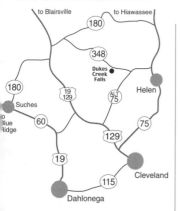

- **Falls is visible from parking area**
- **Fishing**
- **User fee charged**

Whether you'd like to view it from afar or up close and personal, Dukes Creek Falls is worth a look. A looping 1.1 mile developed path descends to the creek at the junction of Dukes Creek and Davis Creek. The waterfall is actually on Davis Creek, and drops nearly 200' from the brink. The area at the base is very scenic, as the waters of Davis Creek merge with the crashing whitewater of Dukes Creek. An overlook in the parking area provides a long range view for those who would rather not hike down, but hey, we all need the exercise, right?

Directions: From Helen, take GA 75 north for 1.5 miles. Turn left onto GA 75 ALT and go 2.3 miles to Russell Hwy (GA 348). Drive 2 miles to Dukes Creek Recreation Area on left.

Helton Creek Falls

DESTINATION **29**

One of North Georgia's lovliest cascades

Chattahoochee National Forest – Union County
Length: short walk over rocky trail with some steps

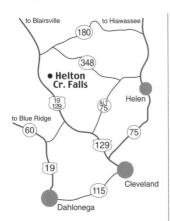

- **Great picnic spot**
- **Bring your camera**
- **User fee charged**

It's a rare treat when one of the area's most outstanding scenic attractions also happens to be very easy to access. That's the case at Helton Creek Falls, one of North Georgia's prettiest, yet relatively unknown, waterfalls. This 60' beauty slides into a picture-perfect plunge pool surrounded by fragrant laurel and rhododendron.

Directions: Proceed 1.6 miles north from Neel's Gap. Turn right onto Helton Creek Rd (FS 118) and drive 2.3 bumpy miles to the pull-off.

High Shoals

DESTINATION 30

Beautiful waterfalls secluded in a cool mountain cove

High Shoals Scenic Area – Towns County
2.4 mile walk (round trip) to High Shoals Falls
Hike is rated MODERATE

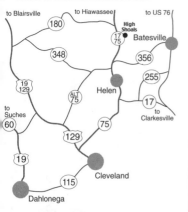

- **Scenic short hike**
- **Great picnic spot**
- **View these cascades from the observation decks!**

Two major waterfalls hidden within a thick grove of beautiful rhododendrons await visitors to **High Shoals Scenic Area** near Unicoi Gap. A looping 1.2 mile trail drops around 300' in elevation from the trailhead to splendid High Shoals Creek. Here a wooden bridge spans the splashing stream, then follows it downstream through an open area great for picnicking.

The blue-blazed trail tunnels through a particularly thick stand of rhododendron before spurring off to the left for a short walk to beautiful Blue Hole Falls. Blue Hole Falls is aptly named, as the 30' sheer cascade drops into a wide, deep plunge pool. An observation deck provides a safe, close-up view perfect for photography.

Returning to the main trail, continue downhill to the next spur to the left. This path drops down to High Shoals Falls, the highest of the cascades in the scenic area. High Shoals Falls descends in a series of cascades for a total drop of about 100', fanning out as it nears the base. An observation deck at the base provides the ONLY safe viewing of this spectacular waterfall.

Probably due to their secluded location, the waterfalls here at High Shoals seem to attract an unusual amount of stupid behavior. It is quite common to see people climbing the rocks alongside the falls and even rock-hopping across the streams along the brink of the falls. There have been numerous fatalities here, so use good common sense and stay on the trails and observation decks!

Directions: From Helen, take GA 75 north for 11 miles and turn right on FS 283 (Indian Grave Gap Rd - 2 miles north of Unicoi Gap). Drive 1.3 miles (warning: bumpy road with a shallow stream ford) uphill to the tiny parking area on the left.

Blue Hole Falls

DeSoto Falls

DESTINATION 31

Series of small waterfalls amidst serene mountain scenery

DeSoto Falls Scenic Area – Lumpkin County
0.8 (one way) to middle falls; 2.5 miles (one way) to upper falls
Hike is rated EASY to middle falls; MODERATE/STRENUOUS to upper falls

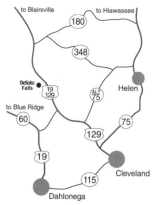

- **Highly scenic area**
- **Numerous small waterfalls**
- **Campground with 24 sites**
- **Fishing**
- **See map on page 47**

History tells us that Spanish explorer Hernando DeSoto came through the area in the 1500's. Legend adds that a piece of Spanish armor was found years later in the area which became known as the DeSoto Falls Scenic Area. Visitors to this 650-acre gem can enjoy camping, fishing and hiking to a series of small but scenic cascades in the Frogtown Creek watershed.

Lower and Middle Falls are relatively close to the parking area and are easy walks; upper falls is 2.5 miles one way, and the trail in the last 1.5 miles is much rougher and steeper.

Directions: DeSoto Falls Scenic Area is located on Hwy 129 about 15 miles north of Cleveland (4.2 miles north of Turner's Corner).

Horse Trough Falls

DESTINATION 32

Beautiful cascade near the Chattahoochee River headwaters

Chattahoochee National Forest – White County
adjacent to Upper Chattahoochee River Campground
0.2 mile (one way)
Hike rated EASY

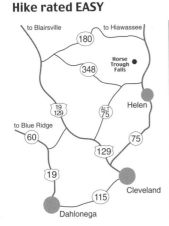

Horse Trough Creek is a small tributary of Georgia's renowned Chattahoochee River, but the 60' cascade found in close proximity to the river' headwaters deserves attention in its own right. Follow the blue-blazed trail 0.2 mile from the parking area to the magnificent 75' waterfall.

Directions: From Helen, take GA 75 north for 8 miles. Turn left onto FS 44 and proceed 4.8 miles to the Upper Chattahoochee Campground on the right. Turn right and follow the road through a shallow creek ford to the parking area. The trail begins here.

- Picnicing
- Fishing
- Camping

Playing in the Pumpkin Patch at harvest time

Section Five

5

Just For the Fun of It

BabyLand General®

DESTI**33**TION

Home of the Cabbage Patch Kids®

Downtown Cleveland – White County
Short walk from historic courthouse and town square

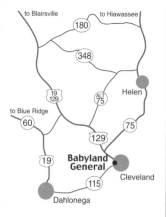

to Blairsville
to Hiawassee
180
348
19 129
ALT 75
Helen
to Blue Ridge
60
75
129
19
Babyland General
Cleveland
115
19
Dahlonega

BabyLand General® Hospital
19 Underwood Street
Cleveland, GA 30528
(706) 865–2171

Whether you're a youngster, or just young at heart, one of the MUST destinations in this part of Northeast Georgia is delightful BabyLand General® Hospital, home of the adorable and world-renowned Cabbage Patch Kids®.

Visitors come here from near and far to adopt one (or more!) of these cuddly kids, some right from birth. Once you've taken the Oath of Adoption, it's official - you have a new addition to your family.

The medical staff is certainly correct here when they say - "This is certainly like no other hospital you've ever visited!"

Gold Panning

DESTINATION 34

At the site of America's first major gold rush

Several locations near Dahlonega and Cleveland

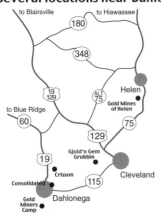

- Consolidated Gold Mines (706) 864-8473
- Crisson Gold Mine (706) 864-6363
- Gold'n Gem Grubbin (706) 865-5454
- Gold Mines of Helen (706) 878-3052
- Gold Miners Camp (706) 864-6373

(check with local Chamber
of Commerce for others)

There's gold in them thar hills! Nearly 175 years after the discovery of gold near Dahlonega, people still come to pan for the mystical, magical metal. There are a number of mines and panning sites currently open to the public for both gold and gemstone mining.

The largest of these is Consolidated Gold Mines, which is on the National Register of Historic Sites, and offers exciting underground mine tours at was reported to have been the largest gold mining operation east of the Mississippi in the late 1800's.

Most of these establishments offer panning instruction, and also feature historic mining equipment exhibits and gem related gift shops. Additionally, some offer contests and seasonal festivals. Who knows - maybe you'll strike it rich!

Mountain Waterworks  DESTINATION 35

Tubing and canoeing on pristine mountain rivers

Bring your own or rent 'em here!

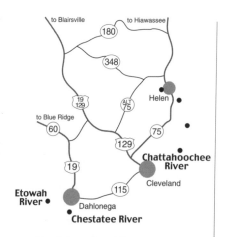

- Chattahoochee River
- Chestatee River
- Etowah River
- See local outfitters for details

I n the middle of a hot, Georgia summer, even the normally cool mountains can get pretty steamy. Not to worry, though, as nature has its own remedy for cooling off - hit the river!

The area around Helen and Dahlonega feature three highly scenic rivers which offer light whitewater action - perfect for beginners in innertubes, canoes, kayaks or rafts.

Chattahoochee River: Hundreds of tubers enjoy the section that flows through Helen on hot summer days. Canoes and kayaks are more suited to the nearly 20 miles Class I-III water south and east of Cleveland above the backwaters of Lake Sydney Lanier.

Chestatee River: Located just east of Dahlonega, the Chestatee offers over 20 miles of easy Class I-II whitewater interspersed with long, placid pools. Suitable for canoes, kayaks or tubes.

Etowah River: Located just a few miles west and south of Dahlonega, the Etowah offers over 15 miles of easy Class I-II whitewater and plenty of splendid scenery. Lower section features tunnel once used to divert river for mining.

Chattahoochee Tubing in Helen: A number of tubing outfitters currently operate in Helen - check locally for names and numbers.

Appalachian Outfitters (Chest. & Etowah)
Hwy 60 South • Dahlonega, GA 30533
(706) 864-7117 Info /(800) 426-7117 Res

Wildwood Outfitters (Chattahoochee)
7272 South Main St • Helen, GA 30545
(706) 878-1700 Info /(800) 553-2715

Etowah Falls (above) and gold tunnel (left)

Classic Shoppes & Eats

Reflecting the heritage and culture of the region

Just a few of the publisher's favorite stops

Eating and shopping, quite frankly, are just as much a part of the Northeast Georgia mountain experience as waterfalls and hiking trails. And when it comes to these two great pastimes, the Helen-Dahlonega area just will not be outdone. Be sure to spend some time in the "downtown" area of both towns, as dozens of fascinating shoppes and restaurants will compete for your attention (and your shopping dollar).

Though certainly not comprehensive, and admittedly quite subjective, the following lists *just a few* of the publishers favorite shopping and dining destinations that offer a special flavor of the mountains or have a unique historic appeal.

DAHLONEGA

The Smith House
It seems nearly everyone has eaten at this world renowned family establishment at least once. Famous for its family-style southern cooking. Also be sure to visit the delightful Smith House country store. Adjacent to the town square.
(706) 867-7000

Dahlonega General Store
Right on the town square. Fascinating old general store featuring collectibles, cookbooks, metal signs, peanuts & jams, old-fashioned candy, etc. all in an old country store atmosphere.

Hometown Bookstore
On the town square. Great collection of local and regional books, maps, posters, flags, historic documents, music, etc.
(706) 864-7225

Burt's Farm

Anyone out in the vicinity of Amicalola Falls State Park needs to head over to Burt's, especially during the fall when over 10,000 pumpkins are offered to the public. Also features gourds, jellies & jams, pop corn, hayrides, picnicking, etc. (706) 265-3701

HELEN

Nora Mill Granary

Built in 1876 on the banks of the beautiful Chattahoochee River, historic Nora Mill features interesting local products such as grits, biscuit mix, bread mixes, syrups, jams & jellies, and much more! 2 miles south of town on GA 75. (706) 878-1280

Old Sautee Store

Located at the junction of Sautee and Nacoochee Valleys, this "country store/museum" is the oldest continuously operated store in White County (circa 1873). Features a Scandanavian gift shop with a fascinating variety of merchandise. Junction of GA 17 and GA 255, 4 miles southeast of Helen. (706) 878-2281

Fred's Famous Peanuts

What shrimp is to Bubba Gump's, peanuts are to Fred's. And that means all kinds, plus honey, apples and cider, pecan brittle, etc. North of Helen on GA 356 - on the way to Unicoi. (706) 878-3124

BLAIRSVILLE

Walasi–Yi

Located on the Appalachian Trail in a historic native wood and stone structure, Walasi-yi features a great selection of books, gifts and apparel, and top-of-the-line hiking gear and supplies. Hwy 19/129. (706) 745-6095

BATESVILLE

Mark of the Potter

Located in the old Watts Mill on the banks of the beautiful Soquee River, this renowned shop features all types of unique crafts and pottery from over 40 local artists. Just a few miles south of Batesville on GA 197. (706) 947-3440

Old Sautee Store

Blue Ridge Railroad

DESTINATION 37

Ride alongside the scenic Toccoa River to McCaysville

Blue Ridge Scenic Railway
241 Depot Street • Blue Ridge, GA 30513
(706) 632-9833 or 800-934-1898
www.brscenic.com

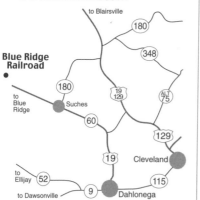

One of the most unique ways to see the mountains is the same way many early tourists saw it - by train. Though you'll have to travel about an hour from Dahlonega, the recently opened Blue Ridge Scenic Railroad is definitely worth the drive. This 26-mile round trip from downtown Blue Ridge to McCaysville runs alongside the beautiful Toccoa River. Normally runs Friday, Saturday and Sunday. Call for schedule.

- **Scenic and historic**
- **Great family activity**
- **Advance reservations recomended**

Scenic Drives

DESTINATION **38**

Mountain highways and backroads offer great sightseeing

Gas up and head out – the open road is waiting!

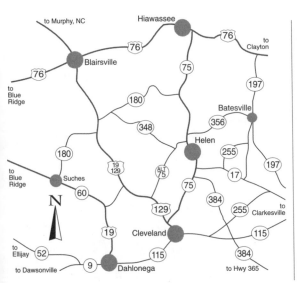

Hit the road! A nice leisurely drive is just what the doctor ordered. There's plenty of good sight-seeing to be enjoyed from behind the wheel (or from a passenger's seat).

While many publications offer exacting routes to follow, (measuring mileage, etc.), why not just take a map and make up your own?

Highways 19/129, 75, and 180 offer particularly scenic drives. Be sure to visit the Richard Russell Scenic Hwy (GA 348) while in the area as well. If you're behind the wheel, enjoy the great scenery, but keep your eyes on the road.

Catchin' the Big One

DESTINATION **39**

Hundreds of miles of mountain streams and rivers

Chattahoochee River, Waters Creek, various streams

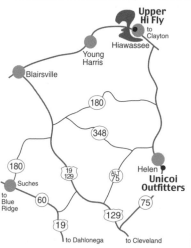

For the sportsman at heart, there is perhaps no more passionate activity than angling for the elusive trout. The Helen and Dahlonega region features hundreds of miles of trout waters containing native brook, brown and rainbow trout. Two local outfitters can help fishermen of any skill level with specialized equipment, expert advise, maps or guided trips, (but you probably won't need any help making up your fish stories).

- **Unicoi Outfitters**
  Helen, GA (706) 878-3083
- **Upper Hi Fly**
  Hiawassee, GA (706) 896-9075

Saddle Up

DESTINATION **40**

Enjoy horseback riding in the mountains...

Several local stables offering a variety of rides

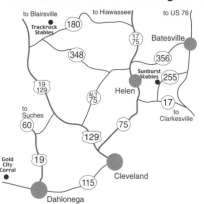

There's nothing quite like experiencing the mountains from the back of one of nature's most nobles beasts. Maybe its in identifying with those early explorers and settlers who relied on these animals so much for their transportation, or perhaps even their vocation.

Regardless of the reason, get off your feet and into the saddle at one of several riding outfitters in the Helen-Dahlonega area.

- Gold City Corral – Dahlonega (706) 867–9395
- Sunburst Stables – Clarkesville (706) 947–7433
- Trackrock Stables – Blairsville (706) 745–5252
- Sleepy Hollow Stables – Sautee (706) 878–2618
- Millstone Stables – Helen (706) 878–1600
- Hornes Buggy Rides – Helen (706) 878–3658
  (some of the parks and recreation areas offer
  horseback riding seasonally – check locally)

Festivals & Special Events DESTINATION 41

Special celebrations of our mountain heritage

Festivals, fairs & special events – partial listing

It used to be in years past that when you spoke of mountain festivals, you were generally referring to those special events which took place in the fall of the year. Mountain fairs and festivals in the autumn were as much a part of life in these hills as Christmas and New Year's.

With the development of the region as a major tourist destination, additional special events now take place on a regular basis year round! Regardless of what time of the year you visit, chances are good that you'll be able to enjoy some type of program, festival or fair in the Northeast Georgia Mountains. Listed here are *just a few* of these special events you may want to try to catch.

Dahlonega

World Championship Gold Panning Comp.
Third Weekend in April

Wildflower Festival of the Arts
Third Weekend in May

Bluegrass Festival
June

Family Days Celebration
July 4th

Gold Rush Days
Third Weekend in October

An Old Fashioned Christmas in Dahlonega
Weekends in December

Dahlonega-Lumpkin County Chamber of Comm.
101 South Park St., Dahlonega GA 30533
(706) 864-311

Helen

Fireside Art & Craft Show
February - Unicoi State Park

Annual Trout Tournament
end of March

Helen to Atlantic Balloon Race
June

Oktoberfest
mid-September through early November

Halloween Haunted Gold Mines
October

Appalach. Christmas at BabyLand General®
November-December (Cleveland)

Helen Welcome Center   White Co. COC
PO Box 730   1-800-392-8279
Helen, GA 30545
(706) 878-2181

Contact the local Chamber of Commerce where you are visiting for a complete, up-to-date listing of festivals and special events.

Hiawassee

Rhododendron Festival
end April - first of May

Spring Music Festival
May

Georgia Mountain Fair
early to mid-August

"The Reach of Song" Appalachian Drama Young Harris College, Young Harris
June - August

Towns County Chamber of Commerce
1411 Fuller Circle
Young Harris, GA 30582

Blairsville

Sorghum Festival
October weekends

Blairsville/Union Co. Chamber of Commerce
PO Box 789, Blairsville, GA 30514
(706) 745-1382

Chattahoochee National Forest

Chattahoochee National Forest – 750,000 acres

Recreational opportunities abound in Georgia's magnificent Chattahoochee National Forest. Encompassing an area of nearly three-quarters of a million acres, the immensely popular Chattahoochee National Forest features nearly 400 miles of hiking trails, almost two dozen recreation areas, hundreds of campsites, fishing and opportunities, and the list goes on.

Named for the Chattahoochee River which rises just west of Unicoi Gap, this area attracts large numbers of visitors, especially in the warmer months. For a detailed visitor map or more information, stop by one of the local U.S. Forest Service Ranger stations.

Dahlonega/Helen Area Ranger District Offices:

US Forest Service
1755 Cleveland Hwy
Gainesville, GA 30501
(770) 536-0541

Chestatee Ranger District
102 Memorial Drive
Dahlonega, GA 30533
(706) 864-6173

Brasstown Ranger District
1881 Highway 515
Blairsville, GA 30512
(706) 745-6928

Chattooga Ranger District
200 Hwy 197 North
Clarkesville, GA 30523
(706) 754-6221

Notes

Notes